LOOK AT YOU

LOOK AT YOU
Copyright © 2023
Wise Experience LLC

SELF-REFLECTION

Noun

Is the ability to witness and
evaluate our own cognitive,
emotional, and behavioral
processes.

A STEP IN THE RIGHT DIRECTION

The purpose of this journal is to provide a safe and non-judgmental environment for you to be honest with yourself and explore your truth.

Looking within and having self-accountability is a step toward being a better version of your true self.

This involves asking yourself questions, exploring your motivations, and analyzing your reactions. Self-reflection can help you identify patterns in your thinking and behavior, which can help you make positive changes in your life.

This journal is a tool for self-discovery, self-awareness, and personal growth.

This journal provides a space to reflect and explore your thoughts, feelings, and experiences.

By taking the time to self-reflect, you can better understand yourself, your values, your strengths, and your goals.

Take some time out, relax, get into comfy clothes, and grab your favorite drink, but don't spill any on the pages.

Please know that this journal is for your eyes only. No one else shall be reading it. Be as honest and open as you need to be. This space allows you to be vulnerable and authentic without fear of judgment or criticism.

OUT WITH THE OLD

&

IN WITH THE NEW

YOU

_____

Name

Take a deep breath and dive in. Trust yourself and your instincts. You are on a journey of self-discovery, and This journal is here to help you along the way.

What word(s) come to mind when I think of my name?

_____

_____

_____

_____

_____

_____

_____

You are purposely made

If I could change my name,
what would I change it to
and why?

_____

_____

_____

_____

_____

_____

_____

You are purposely made

Does my name have a
meaning behind it? What is
it, and do I feel it fits me?

_____

_____

_____

_____

_____

_____

_____

You are meaningful

When I look at myself in
the mirror
what do I honestly see?

_____

_____

_____

_____

_____

_____

_____

You are so much more than what you see

Who do I admire or
look up to and why?

_____

_____

_____

_____

_____

_____

_____

Look up to see your potential

Look up to see your potential

List positive words
that I believe describe
my character

_____

_____

_____

_____

_____

_____

_____

How you see yourself matters

List negative words that
I believe describe my
character.
Ex: Immature,
irresponsible arrogant

_____

_____

_____

_____

_____

_____

_____

How you see yourself matters

What are some things
that make me smile about
myself?
Ex: Helping a stranger out,
encouraging someone

_____

_____

_____

_____

_____

_____

_____

_____

Your smile is unique, like you.

_____

_____

_____

_____

_____

_____

_____

_____

_____

You are purposely made

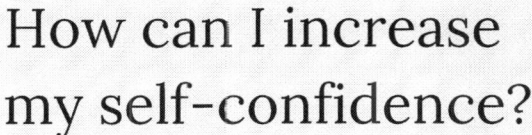

How can I increase
my self-confidence?

Confidence looks good on you

How's my spiritual life?
Do I need to make changes?
If so, what will be my start
date, and what would be the
changes?

_____

_____

_____

_____

_____

_____

_____

_____

Stay connected to your creator

_____

_____

_____

_____

_____

_____

_____

_____

_____

_____

_____

_____

_____

Stay connected to your creator

What are my specific fears, and how did they originate?

_____

_____

_____

_____

_____

_____

_____

Conquer your fears to move forward

Identifying My Trauma Response: Fight, Flight, or Fawn?
Which trauma response do I believe I have?

_____

_____

_____

_____

_____

_____

_____

_____

Trauma is not your fault, but it is your responsibility

Where would I go, and what would I do if I could go back in time?

_____

_____

_____

_____

_____

_____

_____

The past can heal the present and prepare the future

Describe some school memories that stick out good or bad.

_____

_____

_____

_____

_____

_____

_____

School memories collecting moments, not things

Look back over my
answers to the previous
questions.
Do I notice any
commonalities?

_____

_____

_____

_____

_____

_____

_____

It's a different view when the outside is looking in

_____

_____

_____

_____

_____

_____

_____

_____

_____

_____

It's a different view when the outside is looking in

SELF CARE:

NOUN
THE PRACTICE OF
TAKING ACTION TO
PRESERVE OR IMPROVE
ONE OWNS HEALTH

SELF-CARE IS AN
IMPORTANT PART
OF BEING HAPPY.

THIS INCLUDES
THINGS LIKE
GETTING ENOUGH
SLEEP, EXERCISING
REGULARLY,
EATING A HEALTHY
DIET, AND TAKING
TIME TO RELAX
AND RECHARGE.

How and what do
I do to manage
any stress?

_____

_____

_____

_____

_____

_____

_____

Stress is a silent killer that speaks aloud

Am I resting well?
What does my sleep pattern
look like?

_____

_____

_____

_____

_____

_____

_____

Recharge the body and replenish the brain

Am I happy with my appearance? Why or why not?

_____

_____

_____

_____

_____

_____

_____

_____

True beauty starts within

What does my self-care look like?

_____

_____

_____

_____

_____

_____

_____

_____

Self -care brings serenity

How can I take better
care of physical and
mental health ?

It's okay to put yourself first. It's healthy

What books am I reading or planning to read?

_____

_____

_____

_____

_____

_____

_____

Empower your mind

What genre of music do I prefer and what draws me to it?

_____

_____

_____

_____

_____

_____

_____

Try something different

ESCAPE
AND WRITE DOWN ANY
WORDS, PHRASES,OR
SENTENCES THAT
COMES TO YOUR MIND

GRATITUDE

NOUN
THE QUALITY OF BEING
THANKFUL, READINESS TO
SHOW APPRECIATION FOR AND
TO KINDNESS

PRACTICE GRATITUDE:

GRATITUDE CAN HELP YOU FOCUS ON THE POSITIVE ASPECTS OF YOUR LIFE AND HELP YOU FEEL HAPPIER. TAKE SOME TIME EACH DAY TO REFLECT ON THE THINGS YOU'RE GRATEFUL FOR, EVEN IF THEY SEEM SMALL.

What am I grateful for this week?

_____

_____

_____

_____

_____

_____

_____

Gratitude will take you far

_____

_____

_____

_____

_____

_____

_____

_____

_____

_____

Gratitude will take you far

How can or do I show gratitude towards others?

_____

_____

_____

_____

_____

_____

_____

Gratitude will take you far

What are my strengths
and how can I leverage them
more in my life?

_____

_____

_____

_____

_____

_____

_____

Imperfectly perfect

Imperfectly perfect

What are the things I'm proud of that I said or did?

_____

_____

_____

_____

_____

_____

_____

Its' okay to clap for yourself

Can practicing gratitude
help me become more
resilient? If so, how?

_____

_____

_____

_____

_____

_____

_____

_____

Gratitude is the key to happiness

ESCAPE
AND WRITE DOWN ANY
WORDS, PHRASES,OR
SENTENCES THAT
COMES TO YOUR MIND

BOUNDARIES

NOUN
A LINE THAT MARKS
LIMITS OF AN AREA.

What core values and
needs do I want to
protect and honor
through boundaries?

_____

_____

_____

_____

_____

_____

_____

lead with integrity

What fear or beliefs might hold me from setting and enforcing boundaries?

_____

_____

_____

_____

_____

_____

_____

Put you first

What are the positive and negative consequences of having strong and healthy boundaries in my life?

_____

_____

_____

_____

_____

_____

_____

Setting boundaries is self-respect

How do I communicate my boundaries to others, and am I assertive in upholding them?

_____

_____

_____

_____

_____

_____

_____

Setting boundaries is self- love

FINANCE

NOUN
THE STUDY AND
DISCIPLINE OF
MONEY CURRENCY
AND CAPITAL
ASSETS

Am I investing my
money wisely, or do I
need to educate myself
on investing?

_____

_____

_____

_____

_____

_____

_____

_____

**Investing requires patience and effort but can lead to
significant rewards in the future.**

Does my current finances cover my financial goals? If not, what changes can I make?

_____

_____

_____

_____

_____

_____

_____

Plan ahead so you wont get behind

Am I living within my means, or am I overspending?

_____

_____

_____

_____

_____

_____

_____

Live within your means to have financial stability

Who taught me about credit? How's my credit score? Does it need improvement?

_____

_____

_____

_____

_____

_____

_____

Good credit can unlock many doors

What are my financial goals for the next year, and how can I achieve them?

_____

_____

_____

_____

_____

_____

_____

Plan ahead so you wont get behind

Do I have a budget and if not how and when will I create one?

_____

_____

_____

_____

_____

_____

_____

Spend wisely, not freely

Have I saved enough money
for emergencies, unexpected
expenses, and retirement?

_____

_____

_____

_____

_____

_____

_____

_____

Be ready so you want have to get ready

How can I make a positive impact through giving back?

_____

_____

_____

_____

_____

_____

_____

Be the change you want to see

GOALS

An idea of the future or desired results that a person or a group of people envision

What are my goals for
the next three years, and
what steps can I take to
achieve them?

_____

_____

_____

_____

_____

_____

_____

Start where you are

_____

_____

_____

_____

_____

_____

_____

_____

_____

_____

_____

_____

Start where you are

How do I plan on responding to things in the future that may trigger me?

_____

_____

_____

_____

_____

_____

_____

Be intentionally Be Mature

Have I done the
things I've dreamt
of? If so, list some.

_____

_____

_____

_____

_____

_____

_____

Time is precious do what makes you happy

What are my passions and how can I incorporate them into my life more?

_____

_____

_____

_____

_____

_____

_____

Your passion is connected to your purpose

FORGIVENESS

NOUN
IN A PSYCHOLOGICAL SENSE, IS
THE INTENTIONAL AND
VOLUNTARY PROCESS BY
WHICH ONE WHO MAY
INITIALLY FEEL VICTIMIZED OR
WRONGED GOES THROUGH A
CHANGE IN FEELINGS AND
ATTITUDE REGARDING A GIVEN
OFFENDER, AND OVERCOMES
THE IMPACT OF THE OFFENSE
INCLUDING NEGATIVE
EMOTIONS SUCH AS
RESENTMENT AND A DESIRE
FOR VENGEANCE (HOWEVER
JUSTIFIED IT MIGHT BE).

Gain peace and forgive yourself first

What are the
things I should
forgive myself for?

_____

_____

_____

_____

_____

_____

_____

Forgiveness makes room for happness

Who do I want to forgive me
even if they don't know I want
their forgiveness?

_____

_____

_____

_____

_____

_____

_____

No one is perfect

What is it that's causing me
pain and requires my
attention?

_____

_____

_____

_____

_____

_____

_____

Only you can rescue you

HOLDING ON TO PAIN TAKES UP SPACE FOR YOU TO FREELY BE YOU

Who haven't I forgiven, and why?

_____

_____

_____

_____

_____

_____

_____

No one is perfect

FREE YOUR MIND

WRITE DOWN ANY
WORDS, PHRASES, OR
SENTENCES THAT
COMES TO YOUR MIND

RELATIONSHIP

NOUN
THE WAY IN WHICH TWO OR
MORE CONCEPTS, OBJECTS,
OR PEOPLE ARE CONNECTED,
OR THE STATE OF BEING
CONNECTED

The five
Love Languages
♡

Gifts

Acts of service

Quality time

physical touch

Words of affirmation

Love languages refer to the different ways individuals express and receive love. There are five main love languages.

Understanding your loved ones and friend's love language can help improve communication and strengthen your relationships.
It's important to note that everyone has a primary love language, which may differ from others.
(take the 5 Love Language assessment online to find yours.)

List my love
languages in order
from greatest to
least.

_____

_____

_____

_____

_____

_____

_____

_____

Knowing who I am is key

Who needs to be re-evaluated in my life and why?

It's okay to promote and demote people in life

What's a close and healthy relationship that I've been able to maintain? Describe it below.

_____

_____

_____

_____

_____

_____

_____

_____

Relationships are currency

Have I, and do I wish to
rekindle any
relationship? If so, who
and why?

_____

_____

_____

_____

_____

_____

_____

We all have a season and reason in someone's life

Have I destructively ended a friendship or relationship? Why did it turn out that way?

_____

_____

_____

_____

_____

_____

_____

Own your actions

Who and how can I improve my relationship with?

_____

_____

_____

_____

_____

_____

_____

There is room for error and improvement

What qualities and values do I seek in a partner or friend, and am I embodying those qualities myself?

_____

_____

_____

_____

_____

_____

_____

Reflection of me

Are there specific people or relationships that consistently trigger strong emotional responses?

_____

_____

_____

_____

_____

_____

_____

Learn and gain self control

What does my support team look like, and am I satisfied with it? If not, what would I like my support team to look like?

_____

_____

_____

_____

_____

_____

_____

_____

There is power in numbers

Who supports me during my toughest emotional times? Do I give the same support back?

_____

_____

_____

_____

_____

_____

_____

Receive support and give support

Write down my thoughts and feelings on paper. Write from the heart and express myself without reservation. This letter is an excellent way to communicate my emotions.

It's okay to feel

Write a letter to my
parents and express
everything I've
always wanted to
say.

_____

_____

_____

_____

_____

_____

_____

_____

Free your mind

Free your mind

Free your mind

ACCOUNTABILITY

NOUN
IN TERMS OF ETHICS AND
GOVERNANCE, IS EQUATED
WITH ANSWERABILITY,
BLAMEWORTHINESS,
LIABILITY, AND THE
EXPECTATION OF ACCOUNT-
GIVING.

Am I doing the best I can?
If not, what could I do to
feel more accomplished?

_____

_____

_____

_____

_____

_____

_____

Its okay to re-configure

What recurring
patterns have I
noticed in my life?

_____

_____

_____

_____

_____

_____

_____

Cycles are meant to be broken

What is the underlying cause of my emotions?

_____

_____

_____

_____

_____

_____

_____

It's okay to feel

Write down the words
or phrases I wished to
hear in my childhood.
Ex: I'm sorry, I love
you

_____

_____

_____

_____

_____

_____

_____

Hugging the younger you

_____

_____

_____

_____

_____

_____

_____

_____

_____

_____

_____

_____

hugging the younger you

A trauma response is a natural reaction to a traumatic event that can occur in different forms, including fight, flight, freeze, or fawn.

The fight response is characterized by aggression and confrontation.

The flight response involves escaping from the situation.

The freeze response is when a person becomes immobilized and feels helpless.

The fawn response is when someone tries to please or appease the person causing the trauma.

These automatic responses can be triggered by situations like a car accident, physical or emotional abuse, or natural disasters.

Recall and describe a recent challenging situation. How did you respond: flight, freeze, fight, or fawn?

_____

_____

_____

_____

_____

_____

_____

Choose triumph, not trauma

_____

_____

_____

_____

_____

_____

_____

_____

_____

_____

_____

Choose triumph, not trauma

Which trauma response do I have? It may be more than one.

_____

_____

_____

_____

_____

_____

_____

Don't let the opinion of others define you

How have others perceived me, and do I agree or disagree, and why?

_____

_____

_____

_____

_____

_____

_____

Don't let the opinion of others define you

Do I discuss other people's issues or problems with other people? Why or why not

_____

_____

_____

_____

_____

_____

_____

Don't carry other people's weight

What do I do to process my feelings?

GIVE
YOURSELF
PERMISSION
TO
HEAL

Do I tend to forgive easily or hold grudges, and why is that?

_____

_____

_____

_____

_____

_____

_____

Forgiveness brings more peace

What recurring thoughts occur when I'm triggered, and are they related to my core beliefs about myself?

_____

_____

_____

_____

_____

_____

_____

Mature thoughts can help with your triggers

What are my hidden traumas?

_____

_____

_____

_____

_____

_____

_____

It's okay not to be okay

What would I say if
I were to write a
letter to someone
who's hurt me?

_____

_____

_____

_____

_____

_____

_____

_____

It's okay to speak up and express yourself

_____

_____

_____

_____

_____

_____

_____

_____

_____

_____

_____

_____

It's okay to speak up and express yourself

_____

_____

_____

_____

_____

_____

_____

_____

_____

_____

_____

_____

It's okay to speak up and express yourself

When do I find myself
experiencing strong
emotional reactions?
and what are the
common situations?

_____

_____

_____

_____

_____

_____

_____

_____

practicing maturity

Describe my feelings about a childhood memory that hurts me.

_____

_____

_____

_____

_____

_____

_____

Let it out and let go

_____

_____

_____

_____

_____

_____

_____

_____

_____

_____

_____

_____

_____

Let it out and let go

Describe a time I felt abandoned, and in what way did that impact me?

_____

_____

_____

_____

_____

_____

_____

Let it out and let go

Describe a time I felt rejected and how that impacted me.

_____

_____

_____

_____

_____

_____

_____

_____

Let it out and let go

FREE YOUR MIND

WRITE DOWN ANY WORDS, PHRASES, OR SENTENCES THAT COMES TO YOUR MIND

YOU'RE RESPONSIBLE FOR YOUR OWN HAPPINESS

SATISFY YOURSELF

SAY AND DO THE THINGS
THAT EXCITE YOU

TRULY ACCEPT OTHERS FOR
WHO THEY ARE

BE HONEST WITH
YOURSELF

YOU'RE RESPONSIBLE
FOR YOUR OWN
HAPPINESS

NEVER DEPEND ON
ANYONE TO MAKE YOU
HAPPY

What does
being happy
look like to me?

_____

_____

_____

_____

_____

_____

_____

A happier you is a better you

Describe what my ideal vacation looks like.

_____

_____

_____

_____

_____

_____

_____

Explore your mind

What brings me joy
and how can I
incorporate
more of it in my life?

_____

_____

_____

_____

_____

_____

_____

Its' okay to clap for yourself

List at least five fun
things I enjoy doing.

_____

_____

_____

_____

_____

_____

_____

Self -care brings serenity

How can I integrate the things that bring me joy into my daily life?

_____

_____

_____

_____

_____

_____

_____

Prioritizing brings structure

List fun things I wish to do.

_____

_____

_____

_____

_____

_____

_____

Feel free and alive

What is my definition of love, and do I display that to myself and others?

_____

_____

_____

_____

_____

_____

_____

_____

Give love to receive love

What am I thankful for this week?

_____

_____

_____

_____

_____

_____

_____

_____

Express your gratitude

List at least 5 affirmation's starting with I AM

_____

_____

_____

_____

_____

_____

_____

Write it, say it, and believe it

FOCUS ON WHAT YOU CAN CONTROL:

MANY THINGS IN LIFE ARE BEYOND OUR CONTROL, BUT IT'S IMPORTANT TO FOCUS ON THE THINGS THAT YOU CAN CONTROL.

FOR EXAMPLE, YOU CAN CONTROL YOUR ATTITUDE, ACTIONS, AND THE WAY YOU RESPOND TO DIFFICULT SITUATIONS.

What personal weaknesses do
I possess that negatively
impact me?

_____

_____

_____

_____

_____

_____

_____

_____

Look within to heal

Take a moment to reflect on my best traits and characteristics. What are the strengths that make me unique and valuable?

_____

_____

_____

_____

_____

_____

_____

Celebrate your strengths

What's a fun memory of my childhood?

_____

_____

_____

_____

_____

_____

_____

Embrace the good times

What words would I use to describe my life? Express my emotions and how I feel.

_____

_____

_____

_____

_____

_____

_____

If you don't like what you see make a change

What do I do to process my feelings?

_____

_____

_____

_____

_____

_____

_____

Our mental is our foundation

How have I contributed to my community or society?

_____

_____

_____

_____

_____

_____

_____

Giving back goes far and beyond

What's a difference I
want to see in the
world, and how can I
be apart of that?

_____

_____

_____

_____

_____

_____

_____

It's never too late to start

What do I want
to be known for
when I have
passed away?

_____

_____

_____

_____

_____

_____

_____

You can create the life you desire

What are my top priorities and how can I make sure I stay focused on them?

_____

_____

_____

_____

_____

_____

_____

_____

Check-ins are necessary

How can I embody
my values more
completely and
live a more
fulfilling life?

_____

_____

_____

_____

_____

_____

_____

This is your life

What changes have occurred in my personal growth and development over time?

_____

_____

_____

_____

_____

_____

_____

_____

Continue to grow and elavate

Close my eyes. Calm my body. Free my mind. Take a deep breath. Exhale. Write down how my spirit feels.

_____

_____

_____

_____

_____

_____

_____

You are energy

Practice mindfulness: Mindfulness can help you stay present in the moment and reduce stress and anxiety.

Take some time each day to practice mindfulness meditation or simply focus on your breath and your surroundings.

Remember, happiness is not something that can be achieved overnight. It's a journey that requires consistent effort and a willingness to take responsibility for your own well-being. By following these tips, you can start taking steps towards a happier, more fulfilling life.

FREE YOUR MIND

WRITE DOWN ANY WORDS, PHRASES, OR SENTENCES THAT COMES TO YOUR MIND

Remember
You do not have to share your
answer with anyone
, but you can share that this
journal has helped you in many
ways. You can pay it forward and
gift a copy to someone.

Made in the USA
Middletown, DE
21 September 2024

Linking Fact and Fiction in the Great Lakes Lumbering Past

A Teaching Guide based on *Journey Back to Lumberjack Camp* by Janie Lynn Panagopoulos

Jean Shafer, Ph.D.

Contents

Making History Come Alive

River Road Publications, Inc.

Teaching Guide Author

Jean Shafer combines her years of teaching experience and teacher education to produce this unusually creative and thoughtful guide for students and teachers of Great Lakes history. Dr. Shafer obtained her degrees from Ohio State University and the University of Connecticut and is presently an administrator in the Grand Haven, Michigan, school system where she heads a language arts program. She is active in various reading and curriculum associations and has served on the National Study Committee, Literature-based Language Arts, of the National Council of Teachers of English.

ISBN: 0-938682-28-8

Published by River Road Publications, Inc., Spring Lake, Michigan 49456
Printed in the United States of America

The use of stories and novels with authentic settings can help make history come alive for students. The fictional details which flesh out the dry bones of history and breathe lives into facts make the past more real for young people. They begin to see history not as a sequence of events involving a few important people, but as an ongoing process involving people not unlike themselves. Through literature, students begin to recognize the common bonds that join human beings of all times and places.

Because students may lack the background or vocabulary necessary to fully comprehend such historical narratives, they may need support from the teacher to assure adequate comprehension of the material. This guide provides the background necessary for using *Journey Back to Lumberjack Camp* in the classroom. It also provides activities based on a content area theme that has been identified for each chapter. These activities will not only expand students' knowledge, they will also help them to better understand and appreciate the events occurring in the story.

The reading process

In order to fully comprehend material readers must construct, integrate, and check the meanings they derive from a text as they read. These are complex skills that do not develop quickly or automatically. Although some students develop such skills independently, most need assistance and direction in specific strategies that will help them better understand what they have read. A lesson format that will help students acquire comprehension skills is outlined below.

Before reading

Help students understand that all narrative text, from the simplest tales to great literature, has a set of common elements. These include:

- Setting - the time and place in which the story occurs

- Characters - the people, animals or creatures in the story

- Problem or goal - the behavior of the characters in relation to some task that needs to be accomplished or some problem needing a solution

- Events - what happens in the course of reaching the goal or solving the problem

- Resolution - the conclusion of the characters' efforts to reach a goal or solve a problem.

The worksheet section provides a narrative map listing these elements so that students can elaborate on them as they read.

1.

During reading

Students need to learn to monitor and control their own comprehension as they read. You can help them do this by pausing at various places in the story and asking the following kinds of questions:

- questions that encourage students to relate the events in this story to their experiences
- questions that ask them to predict what might happen next
- questions that help them understand the finer points of the story.

Students who are having comprehension difficulties need to develop a repertoire of "fix-up" strategies. Encourage them to read past the difficult spot to see if subsequent information helps to clarify the situation, discuss the story with other students, or ask for help.

After reading

You can help students clarify and consolidate their understanding of a story through the following activities:

- Helping them complete the story map
- Asking follow-up questions that help summarize the story
- Asking questions that help students relate this story to others they may have read
- Providing extension activities such as retelling, dramatizing, illustrating, or writing about the story.

About the Author

Janie Lynn Panagopoulos, a research historian, author, and public speaker has worked in the field of historical research, interpretation, and writing for the past nine years. She began her work in museum education and taught writing in gifted and talented programs. Gradually she turned her interests in Michigan history into articles, books, and programs that have entertained and informed people in all parts of the state.

As a National Historical grants recipient in 1989, Panagopoulos was able to spend large amounts of time in historical research. In 1990 she went on to live what she had learned about the fur trading era of Great Lakes history by traveling down the Grand River with a team of research scientists and educators. Dressed in French colonial and Métis clothing, she retraced the historical fur trading route in a birch bark canoe, investigating historical sites and waterways from central to western Michigan. The expedition was one of a number of "being there" experiences that presentations particularly rich and lively.

As a writer, Panagopoulos has published countless articles in both the newspaper and magazine market. She has written and published four small community history publications and syndicated a Michigan history series that ran in fourteen newspapers throughout the state.

In 1993 Panagopoulos's novel, *Traders in Time: A Dream Quest Adventure*, was published and quickly became a favorite of young readers in the western Great Lakes region, as well as their parents and teachers. It was followed by a second book in the *Dream Quest* series, *Journey Back to Lumberjack Camp*, a rollicking story of a youngster who finds himself in the company of ornery, tobacco-chewing lumbermen of the late nineteenth century.

Panagopoulos's energy, love of history, and talent for telling a good story to both young people and adults, promises to keep her readers happy for many years to come.

Plot Summary

Gus thinks that life is unfair because he has to cope with a troublemaker named Al. But when he wakes up in another time and place after an accident at school, he realizes that his problems have just begun. Finding himself in a remote lumbering camp of the late 1800's Gus learns what life in a lumber camp was really like.

When he is assigned to a job as the cook's helper, Gus finds out just what it takes to feed a hungry crew. He also has a chance to get to know the men and the work they do. But because he's such a greenhorn he has hard time winning the respect of the men in the bunkhouse and holding his own with Alex, the Big Push's son.

In spite of his problems, everything is not all trouble for Gus. Tommy, the camp's Irish barn boss, and Miss Addie, the camp cook, befriend the boy. Even Rat-hole Andy, the meanest 'jack in camp, comes to Gus's defense when he finds the boy has power that few others in camp possess - the power to read.

Gus has still another chance to prove his worth to Alex and the Big Push. When the boys are sent into the woods to deliver the noon meal, Alex's carelessness causes a serious accident. In an exciting episode Gus saves Alex and in the recovery from his own injuries, finds himself safely at home again.

During the last half of the nineteenth century lumbering was a big business in the Upper Great Lakes region. The huge white pines and other trees that grew abundantly in northern Michigan, northern Wisconsin, and northeastern Minnesota became the prime resource for an industry that made a tremendous impact upon the economy and history of these states. Logging camps, sawmills, and boomtowns sprang up through the area, while the vast forests quite literally turned into towns and cities in America's young Midwest.

The great lumbering days of the Upper Great Lakes region provide an ideal study for young students. There are many wonderful legends, tales of adventure, and songs within this colorful segment of history. Many museums in the region display photos and tools from the lumbering past.

The lumbering story also provides excellent examples of how an industry provides many different jobs, both directly and indirectly. It shows how the use of one resource relies on a variety of other resources, such as the need for rivers in transporting the logs from the forests. More importantly, it emphasizes the value of natural resources and the high price of waste and carelessness.

Lumbering days also give students a portrait of America in the late 1800s. Its diverse labor force was a prime example of America's melting pot. The lumberjacks' daily lives provide a reminder of the intense physical labor involved in building a nation. Within this chapter of the Great Lakes past, students see history in the work and play of America's people.

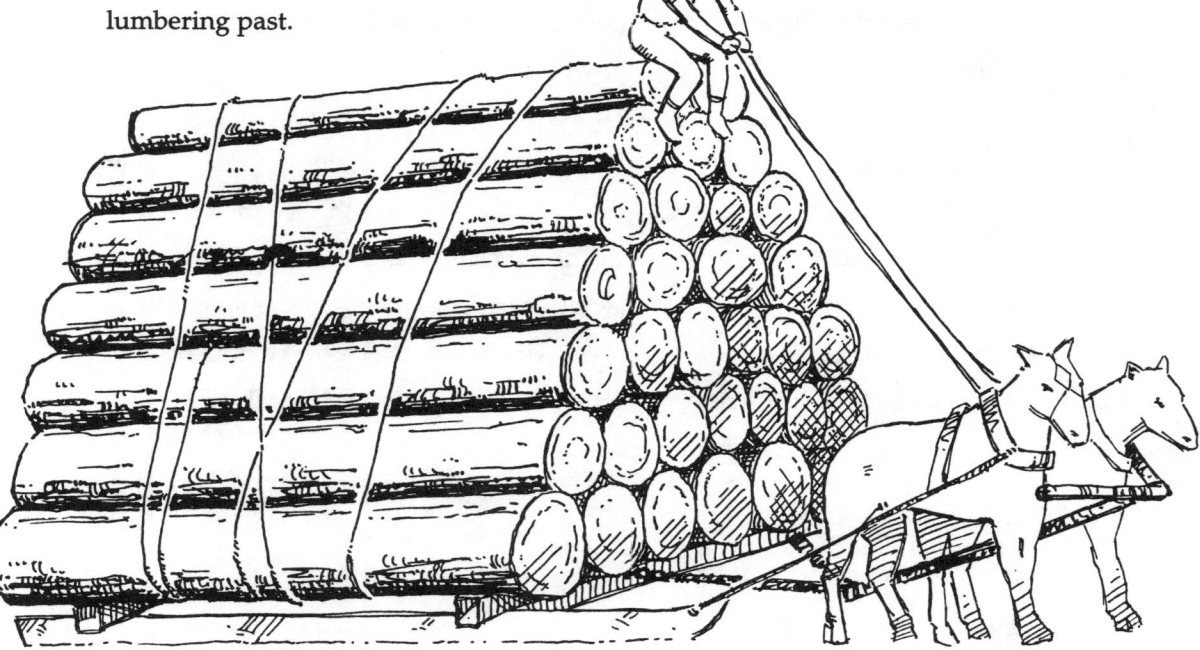

Activities for Students

Chapter 1 • The Principal's Office

Before reading

1. What do the title, *Journey Back to Lumberjack Camp,* and the cover picture tell you about this book?
2. What do they tell you about the setting (time and place) of the book?
3. What do the cover and title tell you about the characters (not just people) in this book?

During reading

1. Where is the story taking place?
2. When is this story taking place?
3. Is the setting of this book the same as you had predicted it would be?

After reading

1. Why do you think the setting (time and place) of this chapter are different than you expected they would be?
2. What do you think might happen with Al's toy gun?
3. At the end of this chapter Gus thinks that he won't have to worry about Al any more. Do you think this is true?

Activities

- Have students begin the *Story Map* on page 18.

Notes

Before reading

1. What do you think the title of this chapter might mean?

During reading

1. What was Mr. Kristie's class studying?

2. Why did he want them to learn about lumbering?

3. How did White Pine School get its name?

4. How much lumber had the state of Michigan produced by the year 1897?

5. When did the Michigan lumbering era start?

6. Why was the white pine a favorite tree of the lumbermen?

After reading

1. What did Mr. Kristie do to help his students learn how lumberjacks lived?

2. Why do you think lumberjacks used strange musical instruments?

3. Why would it have been important for them to have music and songs?

4. Why do you think the saw fiddle was given its name?

5. Why do you think Gus was glad to have Al absent during his attempt to play the saw?

Activities

• Have students add the new characters and setting to their Story Map.

• Have students make a chart comparing the life of a lumberjack with our lives today. Include items such as entertainment, housing, clothing, sanitary conditions, etc.

• Begin to make a class dictionary of lumberjack lingo.

• Teach students the song on the activity sheet, *Lumbering Song* on page 19.

• Have students complete the activity, *Searching for Trees* , on page 20.

Notes

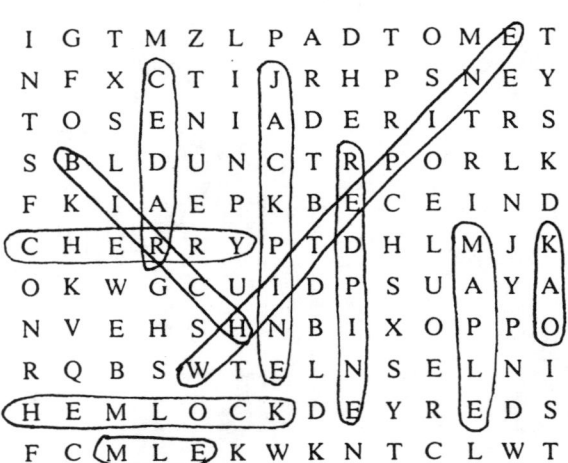

Before reading

1. Now that the author has introduced the main characters, it seems as if she might introduce some problems that they will need to solve or some goal to reach. What do you think that problem or goal might be?

2. What clue does the title of this chapter give you to what one problem might be?

3. Did you have any clues from the last chapter about this problem?

During reading

1. How did Gus happen to catch Al playing with fire?

2. Why didn't Gus just run away from the fire?

3. What else could Gus have done when he saw what Al was doing? Why didn't he do that instead?

After reading

1. Do you think Gus did the right thing? What would you have done?

2. Who do you think will be blamed for causing the fire? What makes you think so?

Activities

•   Have students write a story telling what they would do in Gus's place.

•   Have students add this problem to their story map.

Notes

Before reading

1. What does the title make you think will happen in this chapter?
2. Where do you think Gus will wake up?

During reading

1. Why are there suddenly new characters in this book?
2. How are the new characters similar to the ones in the first chapters?
3. How are the new characters different from the earlier ones?

After reading

1. Where is Gus now?
2. What has happened to him?
3. How do you think he got in this camp?

Activities

• Have students add new characters, major events, and a new problem to the Story Map.

• Make a chart showing how the new characters match the old ones.

• Have students complete the activity, *What's the Chance of a Forest Fire?* on page 21

• Although forest fires are destructive, Nature has ways of repairing the areas after the fire. Ask a group of students to do research on what happens to burned areas and make a presentation to the rest of the class.

Linking Theme - Forest Fires

Among the worst legacies of lumbering were the terrible forest fires that often followed in the wake of the lumbermen. When the lumberjacks finished their work, only stumps and piles of brush called slashings were left. After the slashings dried, a tiny spark could start a forest fire.

The worst year for forest fires was 1871. It was a dry summer. Crops died and streams dried up. In the fall small fires began burning out of control. In northeastern Wisconsin fires destroyed the whole town of Peshtigo. Some say 1,200 people died. Still the fires kept burning. They destroyed other towns and forest lands in Michigan's Upper Peninsula.

On the same day as the Peshtigo fire there was also a great fire in Chicago. Although the Chicago fire received more attention, there were more people killed in the Peshtigo fire.

The story of these forest fires is but one example of the way that people abuse natural resources. One of the important lessons students should learn from history is the responsible use of such resources.

Notes

Answers to the worksheet are D, I, D, D, I, D, I, I, D, I, D, I.

Before reading

1. Where do you think Gus will be when he wakes up in the morning?

During reading

1. How was Gus's morning in the lumberjack camp different than his morning would have been at home?

2   What kind of clothes did Tommy give Gus to wear? What did the other lumberjacks wear?

3. What did the lumberjacks eat for breakfast?

After reading

1. Why do you think the lumberjacks ate such big breakfasts?

2. Do you think all the lumberjacks' meals will be as big as breakfast?

3. How important do you think the cook's job was in a lumbering camp?

4. Why would it be important to have a good cook?

5. What did the lumberjacks call a poor cook? What do you think the name means?

6. What is the attitude about work in the camp? Do you think Gus will learn to do his share? Why?

Activities

•   Add new words to the class dictionary of lumberjack lingo.

•   Have students do the activity, *In the Lumberjack's Kitchen* on page 22.

<u>Notes</u>

The answers are 13, 7, 11, 9, 2, 8, 16, 6, 5, 4, 3, 15, 14, 12, 10, 1.

Before reading

1. In the last chapter Alex said that Gus is dumb. Do you think he is?

2. Why does Gus sometimes do dumb things and ask dumb questions?

3. Why do you think Alex always wants to get Gus in trouble?

4. How does Alex remind you of Al?

3. Why did Tommy say that he had an obligation to take care of Napoleon the bear?

During reading

1. How did the lumberjacks get the logs out of the woods?

2. Why would they haul the logs to the river bank?

3. Why would the teamsters want to keep the tote roads smooth and slick?

4. What are some jobs around a lumber camp other than a cook?

5. Why weren't lumberjacks very clean?

After reading

1. This chapter tells about life in a lumber camp. What do you think you'd like about being a lumberjack? What wouldn't you like?

Activities

• Use the set of study prints *Great Lakes Lumbering* , to help give students a better idea of what life in a lumber camp was like.

• Continue to add to the class lumberjack lingo dictionary.

• Have students complete worksheet called *Moving the Logs* on page 23.

• Have students add new characters to their story map.

Linking Theme - Moving the Logs

Cutting the logs was only part of the job. Once cut, the logs had to be moved to the sawmills where they would be sawed into boards. Considering the weight of the logs, this was no small task.

Typically a team of horses or oxen dragged the logs out of the woods. Then lumberjacks loaded them onto giant, horse-drawn sleds. The sleds could then be pulled along the icy logging roads to the riverbanks where they would wait for the spring rains and snow melt to float them down river to the sawmills. Logging was done primarily in the winter because it was impossible to move such heavy loads on dirt roads or on wheeled vehicles.

The lumbering industry is an example of how critical rivers were to transportation in the early days of our country. With only dirt roads and human or animals to provide power, waterways provided the best means of moving heavy loads.

Often towns and cities grew up along the riverbanks around the sawmills. Later, the advent of the railroad broke our reliance upon water transportation and changed these patterns forever.

Notes - Chapt. 6

Answers to the Logging Match are:

1.	L	6.	R
2.	U	7.	J
3.	M	8.	A
4.	B	9.	C
5.	E	10.	K

Chapter 7 • A Full Day

Before reading

1. Even though the day has just started, everyone in the camp has already done a lot of work. Why do you think there was so much work to be done?

During reading

1. Why do you think the cook's helpers took the food out to the lumberjacks instead of having them come back to eat?

2. Why did Alex have to chop so much wood?

3. Why do you think the lumber camp had a cow?

4. Why did Addie strain the milk?

5. What did the lumberjacks eat for lunch?

After reading

1. Why do you think the lumberjacks ate such huge meals?

2. Do you think Gus will ever learn how to do things right?

Activities

• Have students complete the activity, *Camp Crossword* on page 24.

• Addie said that she was going to make butter from the cream on the milk. Students can see how this is done by following the directions on the worksheet on page 22. You might want to keep this butter to use on pancakes (see Chapter 10).

Notes

Camp Crossword answers are ACROSS: 1. oxen; 3. mess hall; 5. an; 7. choreboys; 9. tea; 10. pie; 11. lanterns; 13. scratchmyback; 15. cook; 16. barn; 17. shed; 19. dishes; 20. pork; 21. rough; 22. tables. DOWN: 1. office; 2. beans; 4. hay; 6. pancakes; 8. bunks; 12. stove; 14. bench; 16. bedbugs; 18. horses.

Chapter 8 • A Greenhorn's Welcome

Before reading

1. How do you think Gus is going to like sleeping in the bunkhouse?

2. How will the bunkhouse be different from Gus's room at home?

3. What does the title tell you about how the other men might feel about Gus?

During reading

1. What did the lumberjacks use for mattresses?

2. What did the lumberjacks do for entertainment or amusement?

3. Why didn't Gus want to chew tobacco?

4. Why did the lumberjacks say they chewed tobacco?

After reading

1. Why were the lumberjacks dirty? What would they have had to do to wash themselves or their clothes?

2. Why would it have been important for the lumberjacks to have rules about how to behave?

Activities

- Have students complete the activity sheet called *What's the Job?* on page 25.

Linking Theme - Rules of Behavior Have Changed

- Ask students to think about how laws and rules of behavior have changed through the years. Have a group of students to do some research on child labor laws and present their findings to the rest of the class.

- In this theme you might also want to discuss how ideas about smoking and using tobacco have changed. Ask students why this has happened.

- We now discourage people from describing and labeling others by their ethnic or racial background. Ask students why this can create conflict and/or be hurtful to people.

- Hazing is another behavior that now has laws to limit it. Have students look up the term and then speculate why there are laws to curb it in our society.

Notes

What's the Job answers are road monkey, teamster, crumb chaser, barn boy, barn boss, cook, axe man, barkeater, and Big Push.

___

Before reading

1. What does the word "lousy" mean in this chapter title?

2. Do you think Gus will have a good night's sleep? Why or why not?

During reading

1. How many different names for lice can you find in this chapter? What is the real name for one of these insects?

2. How did the lumberjack's clean up in the morning? Why didn't they take a shower and brush their teeth?

After reading

1. Why did Gus begin to wish that he was back at home?

2. How did Addie help protect Gus from Alex?

3. How did Tommy make Gus feel better?

4. Do you think Gus is ever going to get get home?

5. How do you think the lumberjacks would like it if they could somehow step into the present?

Activities

• Have students choose one of the lumberjacks and imagine that they had the power to bring him into the present. Have students write an account of their world from the lumberjack's point of view. What would surprise him? What would he like? What wouldn't he like?

• Be sure that Gus's desire to get home is included in the problem or goal portion of the student's Story Map.

<u>Notes</u>

Before reading

1. What does the chapter title make you think might happen in this chapter? Who do you think will be involved?

During reading

1. Why didn't Alex want to help Addie make pancakes?

2. How did Gus finally have a chance to show how smart he is?

3. What caused the fight?

4. Who do you think put the salt in the sugar bowls?

5. What helped to make Gus feel better after the fight?

After reading

1. Why does Gus always get blamed for the things Alex does?

2. Why does Alex get away with things?

Activities

• Have students make flapjacks for the class by reading the recipe as Gus did (see activity on page 26). This might be a good time to use the butter they made earlier.

Notes

Chapter 11 • A Thing or Two

Before reading

1. Do you think Gus will ever have a chance to get even with Alex?

During reading

1. What extra job did the Push give Gus? Why?
2. What did Gus think was the reason Alex put the salt in the sugar bowls?
3. What do you think makes Alex so obnoxious?
4. What did Gus want to do with the boots? Why did he decide not to?
5. What did the lumberjacks like to do in the evening for entertainment?
6. Why did the man who read the story have trouble?
7. Why did the men like Gus's reading?
8. Why were they so impressed?
9. What does Moonshine mean by "the Good Book?"
10. What did the men decide should be done when they found out who put the salt in the sugar bowls?

After reading

1. What do you think the men will do to teach Alex a lesson? What do you think should be done?

Activities

- Lumberjacks liked to tell and hear tall tales. Some of the most famous of these were the tales about the lumberjack named Paul Bunyan. Read some Paul Bunyan stories and then have students try their hand at making up some tall tales of their own.

- One of the reasons some of the lumberjacks could not read may have been because they had come from a non-English-speaking country. Help students understand this diversity that was so apparent in the 1800s by completing the worksheet on page 27.

- Ask students to make a list of reasons why it is important that people know how to read. Have them discuss what life would be like in a country where only a few of the people could read.

Notes

Answers to *Lumberjacks From Many Lands* are: (1) American; (2) Swedish; (3) English; (4) Native American; (5) Finnish; (6) French Canadian; (7) German; (8) Polish; (9) Norwegian; (10) Scotch.

Before reading

1. After reading the title, what do you think will happen in this chapter?

During reading

1. What happened to the boots?

2. Who was responsible for this?

3. Why did Addie try to stop Tommy from yelling at Alex?

4. What happened to Tommy when he finally did yell at Alex?

5. What did the Push tell Gus he had to do?

6. What did Tommy say he would do to help Gus?

7. How did the Push think that Gus and Alex should settle their "problem"?

8. What did the Push tell Tommy to do about Napoleon? Why?

9. What did Tommy do with Napoleon?

10. What caused the accident?

11. What did Gus do to protect himself and Alex from the cougar?

12. Who saved them? How?

After reading

1. Why did the Push change his mind about Tommy and Gus?

2. Do you think that Alex learned a lesson?

3. Do you think he will change?

4. Do you think the things that happened in this chapter will make people change their minds about Gus? How might the lumberjacks see him differently?

5. Do you think Gus feels differently about himself now?

Activities

• Have students use the character analysis sheets on pages 28 and 29 to describe Tommy, Gus, Alex, and Addie.

Notes

Before reading

1. Where do you think Gus will be when he wakes up?
2. Who do you think the hero will be? Why?

During reading

1. How did Mr. Kristie explain Gus s burned hands?
2. How did Mr. Kristie explain Al's injured foot?
3. What other explanations do you have for these injuries?
4. Do you think Al has learned his lesson?

After reading

1. Do you think Gus's experiences in the lumberjack camp were real or just a dream?
2. What is one thing that makes you think they could be more than a dream?
3. What do you think might happen between Mr. Kristie and Gus's mother?

Activities

• Have the class produce a skit based on the plot of the book. You may want to rewrite parts of it in dialogue form for students to dramatize.

• Have students complete the activity, *Have You Thanked A Tree Today?* on page 30.

<u>Notes</u>

The answer to *Have You Thanked a Tree Today* is ecology.

Story Map

Characters

Main Characters

Other Characters

_____   _____

_____   _____

_____   _____

_____   _____

_____   _____

Problem/Goal

_____

_____

_____

Resolution

_____

_____

_____

Events

Beginning   Middle   End

_____   _____   _____

_____   _____   _____

_____   _____   _____

_____   _____   _____

_____   _____   _____

The Shanty Boys in the Pine

Traditional

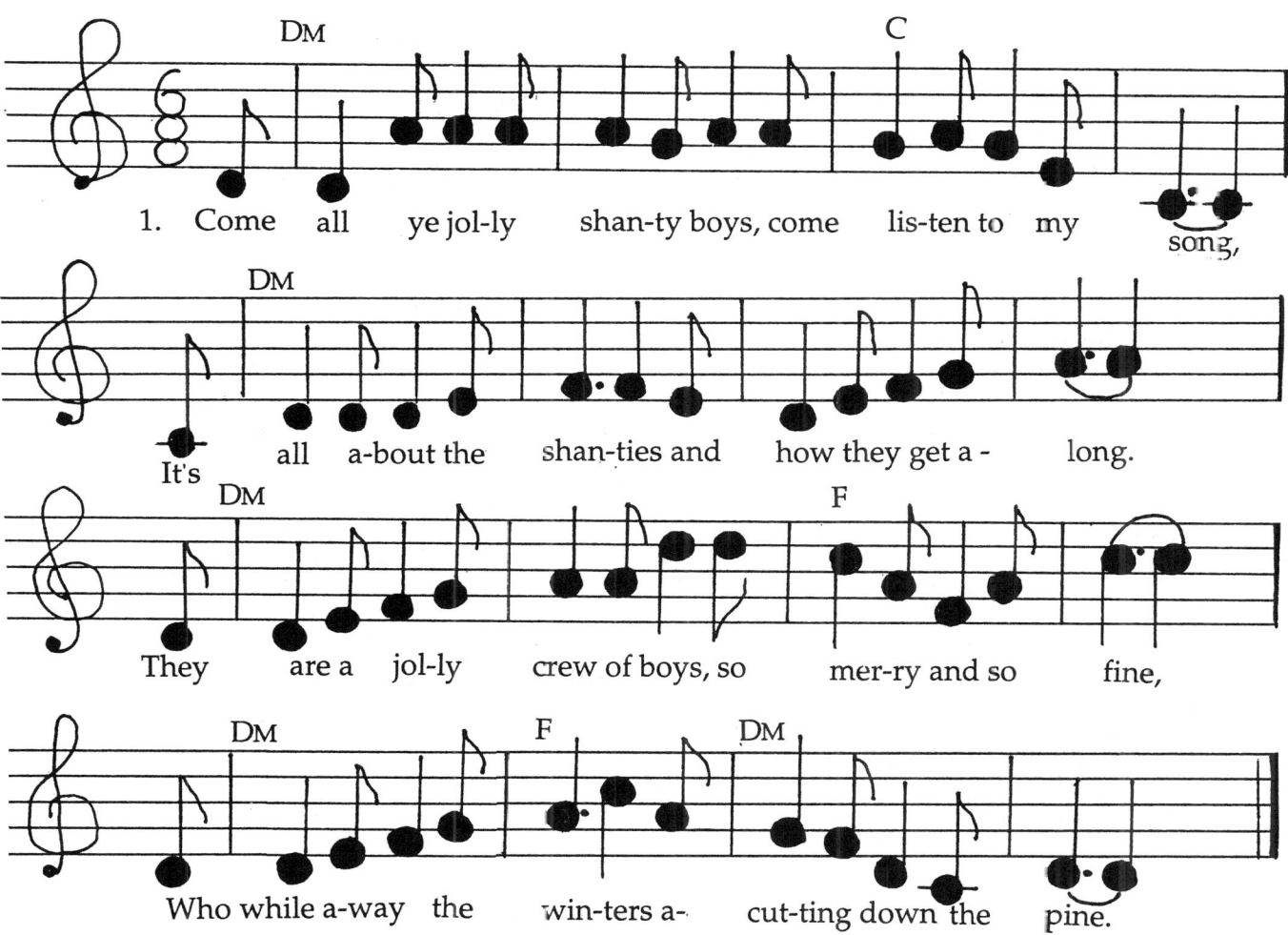

1. Come all ye jol-ly shan-ty boys, come lis-ten to my song,
It's all a-bout the shan-ties and how they get a - long.
They are a jol-ly crew of boys, so mer-ry and so fine,
Who while a-way the win-ters a- cut-ting down the pine.

2. The choppers and the sawyers, they lay the timber low,
The skidders and the swampers, they holler to and fro.
And then there come the loaders, before the break of day,
Come lo-ad up the teams, boys, and to the woods away.

3. The broken ice is floating, and sunny is the sky;
Three hundred big and strong men are wanted on the drive.
With cant hooks and with jam pikes these noble men do go,
And risk their lives each springtime on some big stream you know.

19.

Circle the types of trees that interested early lumbermen. Tree names can read up, down, forward, backward, and diagonally.

I G T M Z L P A D T O M E T
N F X C T I J R H P S N E Y
T O S E N I A D E R I T R S
S B L D U N C T R P O R L K
F K I A E P K B E C E I N D
C H E R R Y P T D H L M J K
O K W G C U I D P S U A Y A
N V E H S H N B I X O P P O
R Q B S W T E L N S E L N I
H E M L O C K D E Y R E D S
F C M L E K W K N T C L W T

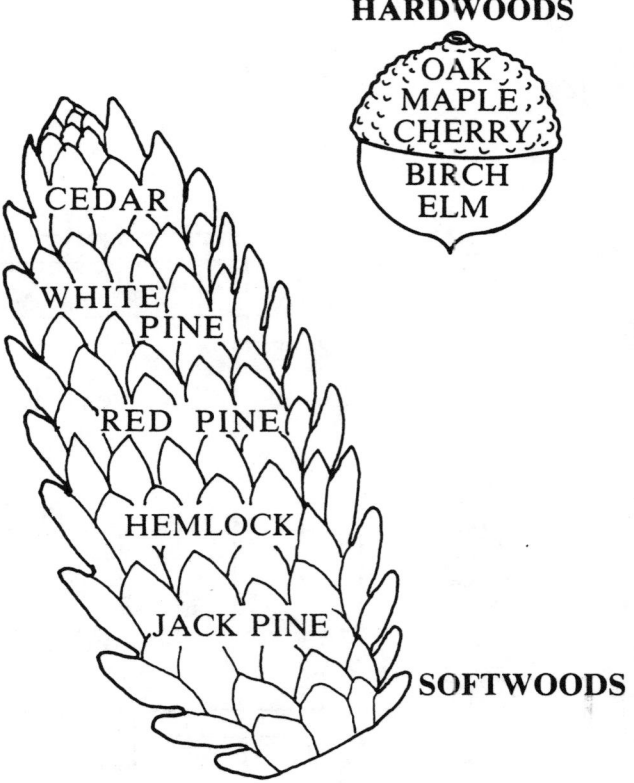

HARDWOODS

OAK
MAPLE
CHERRY
BIRCH
ELM

CEDAR

WHITE PINE

RED PINE

HEMLOCK

JACK PINE

SOFTWOODS

Name the Product

Most of the lumber cut during the great logging days of the Midwest was used to build houses, stores, churches, and other buildings. But many other products were also made of wood at that time. Unscramble the products below, using the pictures to help you.

 sthcole npsi

_____ _____

 hcmta kcssti

_____ _____

 arebrsl

_____

 phsis

_____

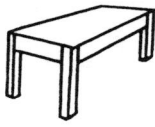 infrureut

_____

 xbseo

_____

20.

When the lumberjacks had finished their work they left behind the dead stumps and branches from the trees that they had cut. When these dried they were a perfect place for forest fires to start—and they did! In the year 1871 two huge fires, the Peshtigo fire in Wisconsin and the great Chicago fire, burned over thousands of acres of land and killed more than thousand people. Today we know more about how to prevent such fires. Test your knowledge of forest fire prevention by reading the statements below and placing an **I** for **Increased** beside the things that increase the danger of fire and a **D** for **Decreased** beside the things that decrease the danger of fire.

_____ It is cool and cloudy.

_____ Farmers clear their land by burning.

_____ Loggers have cut all the trees in a forest leaving only brush and stumps.

_____ A storm is moving through with rains and wind, but no lightning.

_____ Campers leave their fire to burn out by itself.

_____ Forest lands are damp from a long, rainy period.

_____ There has been no rain for weeks.

_____ Lightning is streaking the sky.

_____ Loggers cut only part of the forest, leaving many young trees.

_____ It is a hot, windy day.

_____ Farmers clear away dead brush and stumps with machinery.

_____ Someone throws away a cigarette that is still burning.

Match the lumberjack's kitchen terms listed below with the ones we use today.

_____ dinner	1. kitchen and dining room
_____ long sweetening	2. biscuits
_____ grub	3. eggs
_____ sinkers	4. oven
_____ doorknobs	5. poor cook
_____ jerk the hash	6. a pile of pancakes
_____ pratties	7. sugar
_____ stack	8. serve the food
_____ belly burgler	9. doughnuts
_____ baker	10. pancake
_____ cackleberries	11. food
_____ black lead	12. cook's helper
_____ box up the dough	13. noon meal
_____ crumb chaser	14. knead bread
_____ flappers	15. coffee
_____ cookhouse	16. potatoes

Have a little extra time? You're going to need it if you decide to make butter the old fashioned way.

Recipe for Butter

Bring one pint of heavy cream (whipping cream) to room temperature. Put the cream in a one-quart clear-covered container. Shake, shake, shake the container until the butterfat begins to form clumps. Continue shaking and shaking and shaking and **shaking** until you have a large clump of butter and the remaining milk looks thin and watery.

Loggers not only had to cut the trees, they also had to get the logs to the sawmills to be cut into lumber. Since logs are very heavy, this was no simple task. It was easier to move logs in the winter when they could be loaded on sleds and pulled along icy roads. In this way the heavy logs could be moved to riverbanks and floated downstream to sawmills in the spring when the water was high.

Loggers stamped their own mark on the ends of logs to keep their logs from getting mixed up with logs from other camps. Some sample logs marks are shown below. One log has been left empty so that you can design your own log mark. You might want to use your initials or a symbol in your design. Then complete the logging match below.

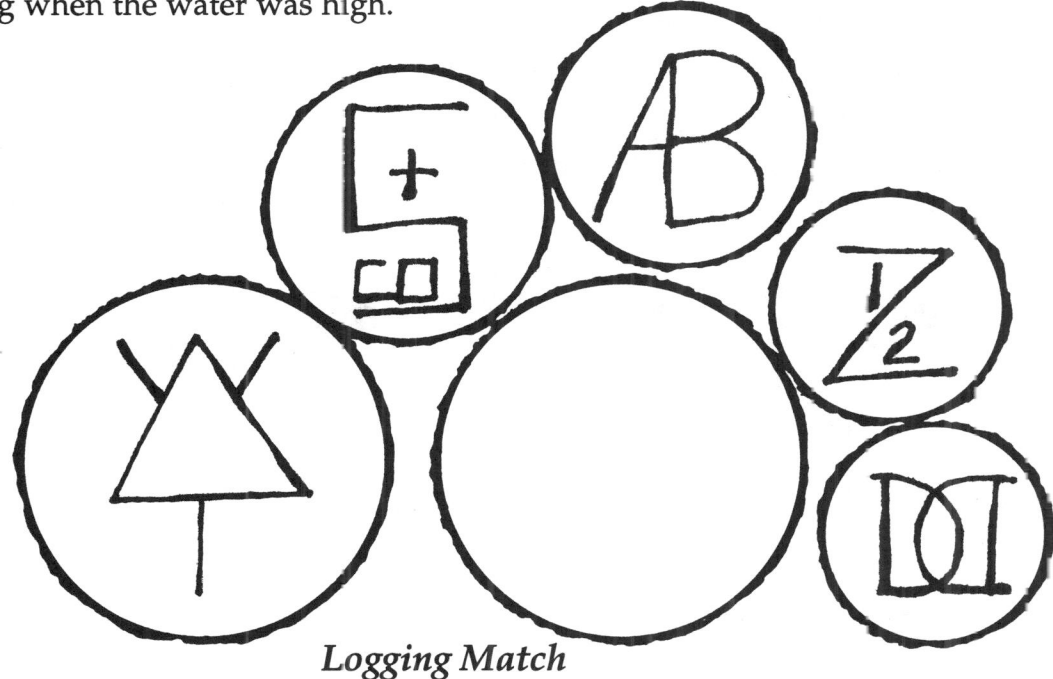

Logging Match

Match the words in Column A with their meanings in Column B. Your answers should spell a common logging word.

Column A	Column B
_____ 1. poor logging season	K. turn left
_____ 2. good logging season	B. used to carry logs in winter
_____ 3. log mark	L. warm winter with little snow
_____ 4. logging sleds	M. a brand stamped on logs
_____ 5. tote road	J. used to move logs in the spring
_____ 6. teamsters	U. cold winter with spring rains
_____ 7. river	A. 1 foot long, 1 foot wide, 1 foot thick
_____ 8. board foot	E. logging road
_____ 9. gee	R. man who drove a team of horses
_____ 10. haw	C. turn right

Camp Crossword

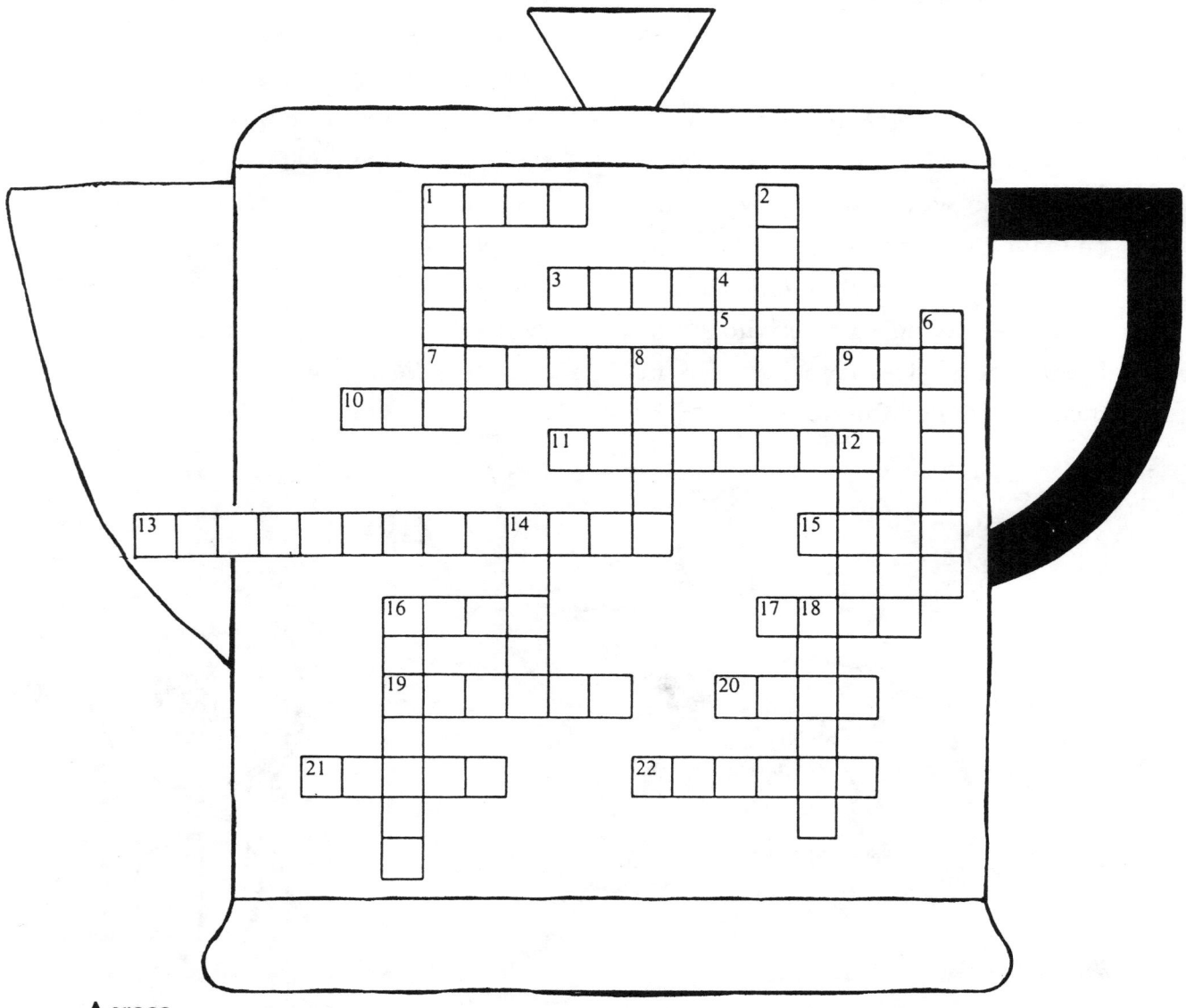

Across

1. Work animals that look like cows
3. Eating place in a logging camp
5. Another word for "a"
7. Helped the cook
9. A hot drink
10. A dessert
11. Gave light
13. Saw fiddle
15. Important person in logging camp
16. Place for animals
17. House for tools
19. Choreboys had to wash these
20. Meat often salted

21. Word that describes camps and rhymes with tough
22. Grub hall furniture

Down

1. Place where boss worked
2. Common food in logging camps
4. Could be used to sleep on or fed to animals
6. Sometimes called flapjacks
8. Lumberjack beds
12. Kept bunkhouse warm
14. Chair for many lumberjacks
16. Can make anyone itch!
18. Kept in barn

24.

Match the following titles with their job descriptions below: cook, barkeater, choreboy, teamster, barn boy, road monkey, axe man, and Big Push.

Responsible for keeping logging roads in good shape. Must be willing to work.

_____

Lumberjacks will respect anyone who can do this job well. Must be an early riser.

_____

Must know how to handle horses. Preferably has their own team.

_____

Someone who can swing an axe with speed and skill. Needs good judgment.

_____

Good job for a person starting out in logging. Must do odd jobs such as dishwashing and peeling potatoes.

_____

If you would rather work at a sawmill than in the woods, this is the job for you.

_____

Get a start in learning to manage horses and oxen. Must like working with animals.

_____

If you have experience and like responsibility, you might want to be the man in charge.

_____

If you have had experience working with animals, you may like this job.

_____

Gus impressed Addie and Alex with his ability to read a recipe. Today we would be surprised if a boy of his age couldn't read. In the backwoods, schools and teachers were often rare. Many people grew to adulthood with very little education or even the ability to read.

Not only did Gus have to be able to read the recipe, he probably had to double or triple it in order to have enough to feed a crew of hungry lumberjacks. Read the recipe below and then double or triple it so that you will have enough to feed your class. Then follow the directions to make a lumberjack breakfast for your class.

Lumberjack Pancake	Doubled Recipe
1 egg	_____
1 1/4 cups buttermilk or soured milk	_____
2 tsp. oil or melted shortening	_____
1 1/4 cups flour	_____
1 tbsp. sugar	_____
1 tsp. baking powder	_____
1/2 tsp. soda	_____
1/2 tsp. salt	_____

Blend egg, milk, and oil. Measure the dry ingredients and sift them together. Add to liquids and beat until all the flour mixture is moistened. (Batter will be lumpy.) Grease heated griddle if necessary. To test, sprinkle with drops of water. When the water sizzles, griddle heat is right. Pour batter into small pools on the griddle. Turn the pancakes as soon as they puff and fill with bubbles, but before the bubbles break. Turn and brown on the other side. Makes sixteen four-inch pancakes.

Lumberjacks From Many Lands

In *Journey Back to Lumberjack Camp*, Tommy and Addie are Irish and proud of it. But the lumber camps in the Great Lakes region were filled with lumberjacks from many different countries and backgrounds. Try to match the lumberjacks below with the correct background, and write the word in the spaces. If you fill all the spaces correctly, you will spell two words that were often used to describe America and its mixture of people.

Finnish	Norwegian
Swedish	American
Scotch	Native American
German	French Canadian
Polish	English

1. My family has lived here so many years I just think of myself as __.
2. I'm __, just like the brain powder (pipe ashes) that Andy told Gus about when he was trying to get the boy to chew tobacco.
3. My people first came here on the *Mayflower*. I'm __.

4. My people have always lived on this continent. I'm __.
5. If I told you what I was, it would sound like the end. I'm __.
6. I come from Canada, but I don't speak English. I'm __.
7. The capital of the country where I lived is Berlin. I'm __.
8. There's a tasty sausage named after my people. I'm __.
9. My country lies in the same part of Europe as Sweden and Denmark. I'm __.
10. When people think of my country, they think of bagpipes and plaid skirts. I'm __.

Character Analysis

Listed below are three characters from *Journey Back To Lumberjack Camp.*. Below each character's name is a trait, such as "kind" or "brave." Mark the area on the scale to show how often you think the character displays that trait. Then give a reason for your answers.

Gus

Trait   **Reason**

| | | | | |
Never   *Intelligent & Ingenious*   Always   _____

| | | | | |
Never   *Mean & Obnoxious*   Always   _____

_____

| | | | | |
Never   *Lonely & Sad*   Always   _____

| | | | | |
Never   *Kind & Innocent*   Always   _____

Alex/Al

Trait   **Reason**

| | | | | |
Never   *Intelligent & Ingenious*   Always   _____

| | | | | |
Never   *Mean & Obnoxious*   Always   _____

_____

| | | | | |
Never   *Lonely & Sad*   Always   _____

| | | | | |
Never   *Kind & Innocent*   Always   _____

28.

Addie/Mrs. McCarty

Trait   **Reason**

| | | | | |
Never   *Intelligent & Ingenious*   Always

_____

| | | | | |
Never   *Mean & Obnoxious*   Always

_____

| | | | | |
Never   *Lonely & Sad*   Always

_____

| | | | | |
Never   *Kind & Innocent*   Always

_____

Tommy/Mr. Kristie

Trait   **Reason**

| | | | | |
Never   *Intelligent & Ingenious*   Always

_____

| | | | | |
Never   *Mean & Obnoxious*   Always

_____

| | | | | |
Never   *Lonely & Sad*   Always

_____

| | | | | |
Never   *Kind & Innocent*   Always

_____

| ___ | ___ | ___ | ___ | ___ | ___ | ___ |
|(1)|(2)|(3)|(4)|(5)|(6)|(7)|

The bold words below are reasons why trees are so important. They are also clues that will help you discover the missing word above that means the study of how plants and animals live together in the world around them.

1. The first letter (1) is in **shade** but not in **shadow**.

2. The second letter (2) is third in **recreation**.

3. The third letter (3) is in **food for animals** three times

4. The fourth letter (4) is in the middle of **animal homes**.

5. The fifth letter (5) is a vowel used twice in **hold soil**.

6. The sixth letter (6) is a consonant we say can be "hard" or "soft" and is one of the first in **store groundwater**.

7. The last letter (7) is also at the end of **beauty**.

Trees and Time

The life story of a tree can be found in the rings. Usually there is one ring for each year. On this tree each ring stands for 10 years. Draw a line connecting the happening with its correct mark in the tree's ring.

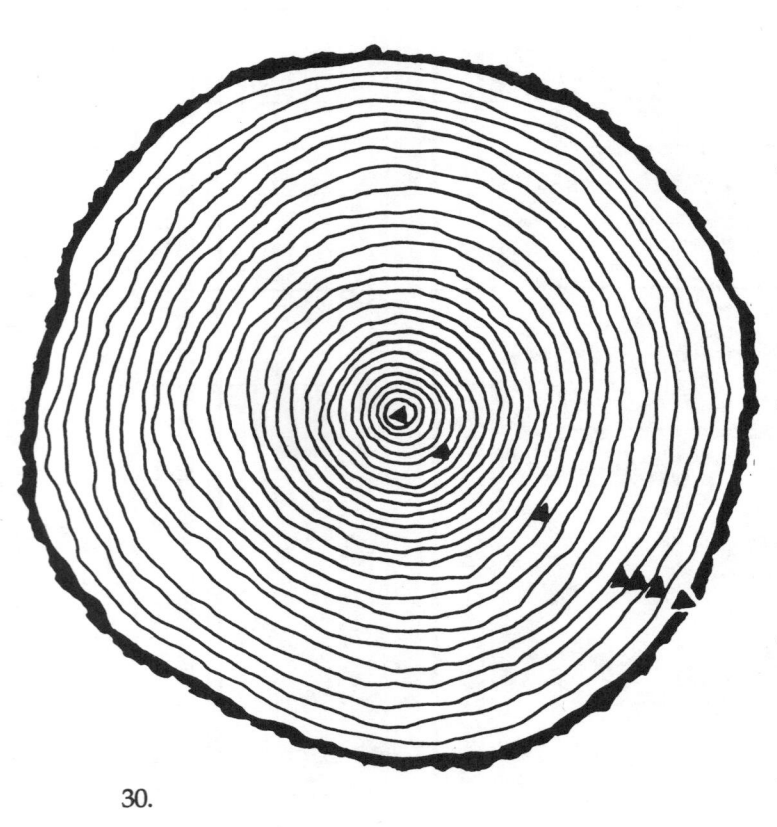

Δ   The tree was very old when Minnesota became a state in 1858.

Δ   The tree was alive in 1776 when the American colonies declared their independence.

Δ   The tree was over 50 years old when Marquette and Jolliet explored the Great Lakes and paddled down the Mississippi River in 1673.

Δ   The tree was still growing when Michigan became a state in 1837-

Δ   And Wisconsin in 1848.

Δ   The tree was just a sprout in when Pilgrims landed in America in 1620.

Δ   A lumberjack cut down the tree in 1870.

30.